Nicaraguan Spanish

Speak like a native!

LEE JAMISON

Visit us at: www.gringoguide200.com

PHOTO CREDITS

To Moraima,
With all my love

Contents

Table of

Acknowledgements

A WORK of this sort can never be accomplished without the help of many contributors. I would like to thank Marco and Alicia Casillas for the office space provided me during the preparation of this volume; Jason Provchy, Paul and Jenny Qualls, and Phil and Luisa Robleto, all for your valuable feedback and corrections; Jorge García and Eleazar Amorrety for clearing up details about some of Nicaragua's most beautiful traditional sayings; and the people of Nicaragua, for their painstaking patience with all of us foreigners who have learned your most lyrical and creative version of Spanish one explanation at a time.

Introduction

WHEN I first visited Nicaragua back in 1994, I was already fluent in Spanish. I had been in an educational work among the Hispanic community for almost ten years and felt proficient both in speaking and writing. But when landing in Nicaragua, I sensed at once that my education was lacking.

Within a short time, I was bombarded with words, phrases, and sayings that left me wondering: "What language do they speak here?" The fact of the matter was, I wasn't bothered by it in the least. It was fascinating to explore this very creative linguistic mixture.

Nicaraguans are a very down to earth people and they unabashedly invent new words and phrases with a penchant, many based on the most vivid of metaphors. Unbound to dictionaries and grammar books, Nicaraguan Spanish is a language of the people, invented by the people and for the people. In them we find jingles and rhymes, a bit of English, a smattering of Nahuatl, references to history, and a sense of family. Resilience and optimism reign supreme. They are a people who have learned to laugh so as not to cry, and they are all the stronger for it.

Are you thinking of visiting Nicaragua in the near future or are you living there now? Do you have family there or from there? Or are you just a language buff? Whatever the case, we urge you: *Join the linguistic party!* Instead of stubbornly holding on to stale textbook Spanish or some computer-generated phrasebook, have an open mind! Embrace those new but yet unfamiliar words and phrases! The more local words, phrases, and sayings you begin to use in your daily vocabulary, the more you will fit in.

The more local words, phrases, and sayings you begin to use...the more you will fit in.

The goal of the *GringoGuide200* series of books is to help you learn the peculiarities of country-specific Spanish. Imitating regional speech in this way dignifies the locals. And even though to them *you* are the foreigner, some may well come to regard you as one of the family. Your efforts will definitely be rewarded —many times over!

ONE SIZE DOES NOT FIT ALL

Undeniably, there is an avalanche of information available on the Spanish language and its grammar. And there's no shortage of phrasebooks. However, the majority of such volumes are exceedingly generic. They exude a one-size-fits-all mentality. Consider some examples:

The generic word for "turkey" is **pavo**. For Mexicans, though, the term is **guajolote**. In Nicaragua, the bird is called a **chompipe**. In Guatemala and El Salvador they say **chumpe**.

In these instances, the generic word is understood. But use the local word and you'll get an extra portion. Not surprisingly, many words that have to do with fruits, vegetables, and meats are very country-specific.

> **We don't teach you Spanish; we teach you how to make your Spanish *more Nicaraguan*.**

The generic word for "orange" is **naranja**, but to Puerto Ricans, it's a **china**. In most places a "papaya" is a **papaya**. But not in Cuba, where **papaya** is a vulgarity. There the correct term is **fruta bomba**.

That's where the *GringoGuide200* series comes in. In this volume, we don't teach you Spanish; we teach you to make your Spanish *more Nicaraguan*, to speak like a native. How? We have made an effort to identify 200 words and phrases that are endemic to the country. We cannot dogmatically state that they are only used in Nicaragua. Words are not stopped by borders, as if they had need of a passport. Nevertheless, *as a group* they are like a fingerprint that unequivocally identifies the Spanish from the land of lakes and volcanoes. For any Nicaraguan who finds himself far from his native land, these words will be music to his hears.

WHY 200?

Check out entry #191 on page 173. There you will find the phrase "**El que mucho abarca, poco aprieta**." It literally means "*he who tries to encompass a lot, squeezes a little*." The idea is that we shouldn't spread ourselves too thin. And that's precisely why 200 words and phrases learned well are far better than an encyclopedia of terms of which we barely scratch the surface.

There is another consideration as well. My mother tongue is English and I have perused many books on English words and sayings. And you know what? A large portion of those words and sayings *I have never heard in my entire lifetime! Never!* The same happens with native Spanish phrasebooks; some are virtual encyclopedias of data. But how do you know if that phrase was known and used by 100 people or a 100,000? *GringoGuide200* saves you the time by sorting that out for you. We are handing it to you on a plate, to practice and to enjoy.

HOW TO USE THIS BOOK

Nicaraguan Spanish: Speak like a native! is divided into 16 sections. Don't feel you have to start at the beginning. Check out the table of contents and dive into the section that most interests you. Others read just one entry a day and then try to practice that new word or phrase at some point during the day. That way you *own* it.

Only one or two words or phrases appear on each page. This will help your focus. For many of the entries a literal meaning is provided. This often sounds unnatural in English, but can be an aid to memory. Furthermore, where the headings "In a nutshell" appear, explanations are given to help you understand the origin behind many of the popular sayings that make Nicaraguan Spanish such a delight to listen to. Sometimes tips are given as to when using that phrase would be appropriate. Just a few pronunciations are provided for words that may initially throw foreigners for a loop.

In the main text, Nicaraguan words and phrases appear in **bold type**. Shortly thereafter the translation of the phrase will appear in *italics*. Most terms have samples of their use in actual speech. In many cases, the words were ripped right from the headlines or newspaper articles that have appeared in the Nicaraguan press. *GringoGuide200* merely collects these quotes and they do not represent the opinion of the author.

Having understood this, "**¡Aproveche Macario, esto no es diario!**" (See page 3.) Dive in and enjoy!

A**Conversation** PIECE

Don't be shy! Break the ice! Check out #1-25 and you will be on your way to speaking like a Nicaraguan!

Al mejor mono se le cae el zapote.

Literal meaning: Even the best monkey sometimes drops the sapodilla.

In a nutshell: The sapodilla, locally known as the **zapote**, is a large, sweet fruit. Monkeys love them. But even an able-handed primate has been known to drop one from time to time. Hence, this is the equivalent of: "*Nobody's perfect.*"

"Este desacierto pone en evidencia que '**al mejor mono se le cae el zapote**,' que somos humanos y nos equivocamos." Translation: "This miscalculation makes it clear that '*nobody's perfect.*' We are humans and we make mistakes."

2

Aproveche Macario, esto no es diario.

Literal meaning: Take advantage Macario, this isn't every day.

In a nutshell: Try this: the next time you offer food to someone and you notice that they are reluctant to accept, rifle off this hearty saying. It's similar to "*strike while the iron's hot*" or "*this offer ends today*." Since it rhymes in Spanish, you'll bring a smile to your friend's face. It is especially used when encouraging someone to take advantage of a bargain. In Guatemala some people say: "Aproveche Matías, esto no es de todos los días." Same idea.

brizar

to drizzle

As an English speaker, when you hear the word "breeze," you think of a pleasant gust of wind. But don't think this word is related. For a local it means, "It's *drizzling*." In most Latin countries they would say "está **lloviznando**."

chagüite

(pronounced chah-WEE-tay)

the plaintain plant

"Pasáme esa hoja de **chagüite**." Translation: "Hand me that *plaintain* leaf." (Did you notice that strange verb conjugation **pasáme**? That's the **vos** form. Unfamiliar with it? Check out **vos** on pages 22-24.) On the other hand, figuratively it means a speech of some kind, a lecture, or a sermon. "Hoy nuestro profesor nos dio el mismo **chagüite** de siempre." Translation: "Today our teacher gave us the *same old lecture*."

4

"Bueno," dijo la mula al freno, "entre más grande, más bueno."

Literal meaning: "Well," said the mule to the bit, "the bigger, the better."

In a nutshell: Pity the poor mule! She must carry her heavy load day by day and is guided to wherever her master desires by means of a steel bit in her mouth. If that bit is small, it will cut into her mouth and create a nasty sore! So, "*the bigger, the better.*" A larger bit is more comfortable.

This nonsensical rhyme is used during conversation after someone has finished a sentence with the word "bueno." It is similar to when in English someone says "Well..." and the other person responds: "That's a deep subject."

cara o sol

Literal meaning: face or sun

In a nutshell: Many years ago the Nicara-guan córdoba coin had the face of Francisco Hernández de Córdoba on the front and the sun on the back. (See photo, back cover.) To make a decision of little importance, then, a coin was flipped and the interested party had to call "face" or "sun." It is the Nicaraguan version of "*heads or tails*."

chapa

an earring

This local term varies from the generic Spanish **arete**. "¡Qué bonitas tus **chapas**! Translation: "I love your *earrings*!"

chunche

thingamagig

If you only learn one word from this entire volume, *learn this one!* It means that whatchamacallit, or thing. It is an awesome word because it can rescue you from those awkward moments when you can't think of the specific word for a particular object. Imagine, for example, that you want your Nicaraguan friend to pass you the remote control to the TV, but you have no idea of how to say "remote control" in Spanish. Just say: "Pasáme ese **chunche**." Translation: "Pass me that *thingamagig*."

PUCKER WHEN YOU POINT!

For a really authentic experience, press your lips together like you are going to pucker to kiss someone and use those luscious pointers of yours to signal the general direction of the object you are talking about. If you can master that technique, you have definitely gotten your investment out of this book and have become a *bona fide* Nicaraguan!

cuecho

This Nahuatl-based word originally meant "something ground." In time, it figuratively came to mean "gossip," similar to the idiom "chewing the fat" in English. Try this: if you see two locals talking to each another, walk by and say with a smile: "**¡Eso es puro cuecho**!" That's like saying: "*I know what you two are gossiping about!*" You'll be on your way to becoming 100% **pinolero**. (If you don't know what that means, see page 114.)

GERTIE THE GOSSIP

Carlos Mejía Godoy, Nicaraguan folk singer, has one song about a certain "Tula Cuecho." "Tula" is the nickname for women named Gertrudes, so "Tula Cuecho" is "Trudy the Gossip." Part of the lyrics go like this: "Tan larga es la lengua de la Tula Cuecho, que cuando la saca y la desempaca, le llega hasta el pecho." Translation: "*So long is the tongue of the Gertie the Gossip, that when she takes it out and unpacks it, it stretches down to her bosom.*" That's one long tongue! Yikes!

de un solo

Literal meaning: at once

In a nutshell: In most countries you would probably have to say "de una sola vez" to express this idea. "Me pagaron mi salario del mes **de un solo**." Translation: "They paid my salary for the month *all at once*."

de viaje

Literal meaning: to be on a trip, to be traveling

In a nutshell: While this phrase can be used in the typical sense when someone is traveling, more often than not it is employed to mean "*completely, totally*." For example, "Él se volvió loco **de viaje**." Translation: "He went *completely* crazy."

en una sola

Literal meaning: in one

In a nutshell: This refers to a unique action carried out in a particular moment and serves as an intensifier.

"Estaban **en una sola** platicadera." Translation: "They were *really talking up a storm*." "Chepito y su novia estaban **en una sola**." Translation: "Chepito and his girlfriend *were making out like nobody's business*." In this last case, the context suggests the meaning.

entre camagua y elote

Literal meaning: Between a tender corn shoot and the cob.

In a nutshell: When corn is neither tender nor completely ripe, it is in this stage. So the intended meaning is to be "*doubtful, or unsure*" about something.

By extension, some use it as a substitute for "*so so.*"
"¿Cómo estás?"
"**Entre camagua y elote**."
Translation: "How are you?"
"*So, so.*"

hacer un volado

Literal meaning: to do a flyover

In a nutshell: To do a favor. If someone says to you: "**Hacéme un volado,**" they will then specify what they want you to do for them: lend them money, run an errand, or buy them something to eat. Hmm, by the way, could you do me a favor?...

No hay falla.

Literal meaning: There is no defect.

In a nutshell: This is a very Nicaraguan way of saying "*No problem*." You accidentally step on someone's toes and, horrified, say: "¡Ay! Lo siento" (*Oh, I'm so sorry!*). And the offended responds with: "**No hay falla.**" Translation: "*Don't worry about it.*"

12

llover sapos y culebras

Literal meaning: to rain toads and serpents

In a nutshell: Many foreign students of English are taken aback when they first hear our very colorful metaphor, "It's raining cats and dogs." You can't literally say this in Spanish, because it won't make sense. However, in Nicaragua, you have this reptilian option.

"Tuvimos que correr rápido al bus, porque estaba **lloviendo sapos y culebras**." Translation: "We had to run quickly to the bus, because *it was raining cats and dogs*."

meter la cuchara

Literal meaning: to stick the spoon in

In a nutshell: They say that too many cooks in the kitchen spoil the soup. While you are cooking, do you really want someone else sticking their spoon in to stir the pot? This popular idiom means "*to enter a conversation without being invited.*"

"Cuando estoy hablando con mis amigos en casa, mi mamá siempre trata de **meter la cuchara**." Translation: "When I'm talking with my friends at home, my mom always tries to *butt in.*"

14

¿oíste?

Literal meaning: Did you hear?

In a nutshell: The first time I visited Nicaragua, it struck me as odd that in daily conversation a good number of sentences ended with "**¿oíste?**," that is, "*did you hear?*" I remember thinking to myself: "Of course I heard. Why do people keep asking me if I heard? Do they think I am hearing impaired?" In time, though, I realized they really meant "*OK?*"

For example, a mother tells her son: "Acordáte de comprar las tortillas, **¿oíste?**". She is merely saying: "Remember to buy the tortillas, *OK?*".

Otro gallo cantará.

Literal meaning: Another rooster will crow.

In a nutshell: In Nicaragua there's no law against having farm animals even in major cities. So don't be surprised at 5 a.m. if you are startled out of bed with a hair-raising cock-a-doodle-do! Hearing the rooster's crow is definitely commonplace. But when someone says "**Otro gallo cantará**," they mean: *"That's another story."*

In a story about the U.S. elections, a journalist wrote: "Si los republicanos ganan la elección de noviembre próximo, **otro gallo cantará.**" Translation: "If the Republicans win the election this coming November, *things are going to be different.*"

peperepé, paparapá

In a nutshell: This is the equivalent of blah, blah, blah with emphasis on the *blah*! Or maybe for you it's *yadda, yadda, yadda.* It usually comes after a long list of things that someone begrudgingly has to do.

For example, "Me dijo que tuvo que ir al banco, luego a la policía, después ir a sacar fotocopias, **peperepé, paparapá**." Translation: "He told me he had to go to the bank, then to the police station, make photocopies, *yadda, yadda, yadda.*"

quedito

This term is derived from the verb **quedar-se**, which means "*to stay.*" But as an adjective it has come to mean "*tranquil, still, or silent.*"

"Cuando el perro estaba ladre y ladre, le regañaron, y se quedó **quedito**." Translation: "When the dog was barking up a storm, they chewed him out, and he *calmed down*."

The word can also be applied to humans. "Yo ya había rezado **quedito**, yo sola para mí no más, sin que nadie me oyera." Translation: "I had already prayed *silently*, just to myself, without anyone hearing me."

Si no es Juana, es Chana.

Literal meaning: If it's not Juana, it's Chana.

In a nutshell: This is the equivalent of "If it's not one thing, it's another." "Cuando Roberta escuchó que había llegado la factura de la luz, gimió: '**Si no es Juana, es Chana.**'" Translation: "When Roberta heard that the light bill had come, she groaned: *'If it's not one thing, it's another.'*" For extra credit, add this twist: "**Y si no es la Chana, es su hermana.**"

THE MARTHA

A curious feature of Nicaraguan Spanish is the custom of placing a definite article in front of female names. "¿Dónde está *la* Marta?" Translation: "Where is Martha?" With male names, no definite article is used.

23

Te fuiste tiste,
y ni adiós dijiste.

Literal meaning: You left, tiste, and you didn't even say goodbye.
(Boy, does that sound corny!)

In a nutshell: Tiste is a drink of cooked corn, but this silly rhyme is used to punctualize an event of small importance. For example, a photographer may say these words to a group after he has snapped their picture. (See also "**Muerta la lora y que nadie la llore**," page 175.)

¡Va pues!

Literal meaning: Go then!

The universal term for agreement.
Person A: "Nos vemos mañana
a las cuatro de la tarde."
Person B: "**¡Va pues!**"
Translation:
Person A: "We'll see you tomorrow
at four in the afternoon."
Person B: "*OK.*"
For extra credit, don't
pronounce the final s,
"**¡Va pue...!**"

VA PUE...

In everyday speech Nicaraguans typically cut off the final s of this expression and many others. You are likely to hear "rice and beans" spoken as "arro' y frijole'." A mother who fears her child is going to miss the bus may shout: "Apúrate vo'. Va' a perder el bu'."

vos

you (familiar form)

If you learned Spanish in high school or college, in all likelihood you were never taught about **vos**. This is a local substitution for "tú," but it has so much more personality! **Vos** is the pronoun for "*you*," but it is only used among close friends. You can definitely feel free to utilize it when talking to children.

But getting your Nicaraguan friends to use it with you will take some effort. Why? They often view foreigners with so much respect that they may feel uncomfortable calling you **vos**. To aid the process, you have to ask them to do it. It's like when you go over to someone's house, walk through the door, but you don't want to sit down until your host invites you to do so. The same happens with **vos**. It doesn't come automatically. In fact, the locals say to use it with you, they need to have **confianza**. This last word means "*an intimate trust*." It means they have to feel comfortable with you. To aid them, you might say: "Por favor, **vocéame**." Translation: "Please, *use the pronoun 'vos' when you talk to me*."

vos

(continued)

If you master the use of this pronoun, you will really fit in with the locals. This means, though, that you have to learn a few new verb conjugations. For example, the subjunctive or command form of verbs as well as the present tense is different with **vos**. Notice the following table that compares the "usted" form with **vos**.

Subjunctive Tense		
"Usted" form	*"Vos" form*	*Translation*
Ande, báñese usted.	Andá, bañáte	Go take a bath.
Dígale a su mamá.	Decíle a tu mamá.	Go tell your mother.
Oígame.	Oíme.	Listen. (Hey!)

Present Tense	
Vos hablás.	You talk.
Vos creés.	You think.
Vos tenés.	You have.
Vos sos.	You are.

vos

(continued)

As you can see, the conjugation of the present tense is similar to the "tú" form except that the accent is always on the last syllable. Notice, too, that in irregular verbs like "tener" and "decir," the verb suffix is removed and "és" and "ís" are added respectively.

To master the use of **vos**, listen in as mothers bark commands at their children. You will hear these verb forms again and again in Nicaragua. Practice them until they roll off your tongue.

Word
OF CAUTION

Be careful! It's dangerous out there! Numbers 26 to 34 will keep you safe!

SECTION 2

A cada chancho le llega su sábado.

Literal meaning: For every pig his Saturday will come.

In a nutshell: In years past, it seems that Saturday was the day when a fattened pig would be taken to the slaughterhouse. For the poor pig, Saturday meant death. So today when someone gets his "just desserts" for misconduct, this saying enters into play.

Commenting on an article that reported the demise of Osama bin Laden, one man wrote: "**¡A cada chancho le llega su sábado!** Solo es cuestión de tiempo para que todos los psicópatas paguen por lo que han hecho." Translation: "*Each person will eventually have his day of reckoning.* It's only a question of time that all psychopaths will have to pay for what they have done."

26

andar chiva

Literal meaning: to walk like a female goat

In a nutshell: *To be very alert.* "Si vas al Mercado Oriental, ¡tenés que **andar chiva**!" Translation: "If you go to the Oriental Market [in a high crime area of Managua], *be very careful!*"

In a slightly different context, **chiva** can mean *dangerous*. For example: "Cuando la cosa se pone **chiva**, hay que alejarse." Translation: "When the situation gets *dangerous*, you have to get out of there."

28

como carreta en bajada

Literal meaning: like a cart going downhill

In a nutshell: Typically, powerful oxen pull carts laden with firewood or other objects. If the cart is loaded and going downhill, the driver must make sure that the animals proceed with utmost caution. If not, the situation will get out of control. If someone, then, is said to be like a **carreta en bajada**, it means that he probably has made rash decisions to his detriment and there is no turning back.

"Con ese noviazgo, Yolanda va **como carreta en bajada**." Translation: "With that courtship, Yolanda is *headed for disaster and there is no turning back*." Likely, Yolanda is going to marry someone worthless and won't listen to counsel. This is similar to "a bull to the slaughter."

Cuando el río suena, piedras trae.

Literal meaning: When the river cries out, it is bringing rocks.

In a nutshell: During heavy rains the river's increased water volume becomes a mighty force, capable of moving even the largest of rocks. All of this, of course, can bring the decibel levels to a thunder. The implication is that *rumors often have some truth to them*.

One blogger, commenting on reports of corruption in one City Hall, wrote: "**Cuando el río suena piedras trae**, esperemos las informaciones oficiales del consejo municipal... Dejemos los comentarios políticos para cuando corresponda." Translation: "*Where there's smoke, there's fire.* But let's wait for official word from City Hall. Let's put aside any political commentary until the appropriate time."

dar atol con el dedo

Literal meaning: to give out atol (a cooked corn drink) with your finger

In a nutshell: Atol is a rather thick drink made with ground corn that has been cooked. Since it is a liquid, it would be impossible to offer it to people with your finger. Scam artists, of course, are always promising to deliver the impossible. Hence, **dar atol con el dedo** means *"to cheat or swindle."*

"Ese vendedor me quiso **dar atol con el dedo**. ¡Venden lo mismo en el centro por la mitad del precio!" Translation: "That salesman was trying t*o pull the wool over my eyes.* They sell the same thing downtown for half the price!"

El papel aguanta todo lo que le pone.

Literal meaning: Paper can take all you put on it.

In a nutshell: This is the catchphrase of the skeptic. He is basically saying anyone can write something down on paper; that doesn't mean that it is true.

One commentator wrote: "**El papel aguanta lo que le ponen**, solo son letras y bla, bla, los que más hablan, los que más critican, son aquellos que están cómodamente sentados en sus oficinas y en sus casas, que detestan al pobre y, por ende, no hacen nada para mitigar la pobreza." Translation: "*People can write whatever they want.* It's just blah, blah, blah. Those who talk the most and who criticize the most are those who are sitting comfortably in their homes and offices, who hold the poor in disdain and, therefore, do nothing to mitigate poverty."

El que se quema con la leche, hasta la cuajada sopla.

Literal meaning: He who gets burned with milk will even blow on cheese.

In a nutshell: In rural Nicaragua, where cattle are abundant, many farmers drink hot milk in the morning with their breakfast. Of course, if they don't blow on their first sips of milk, they can burn their mouths. After that, they could become so *gun shy* that they would go to the extreme of blowing on **cuajada,** which is a type of cheese that is always served cold.

The person who has been burned by some unpleasant prior experience becomes *gun shy*, or **sicosiado**, in the vernacular. For example, "Desde que chocó su carro, Juan prefiere caminar a la escuela. **El que se quema con la leche, hasta la cuajada sopla**." Translation: "Since he wrecked his car, Juan prefers to walk to school. He's a little *paranoid*."

En la boca del horno se quema el pan.

Literal meaning: In the mouth of the oven, the bread is burned.

In a nutshell: Imagine the hard-working baker who awakes in the wee hours of the morning to prepare his dough, lets it rise for hours, then separates the individual loaves and puts them in the oven. At that point, he's got a lot of time invested.

How will he feel if at the last minute he gets distracted and his precious bread goes up in smoke? This adage reminds us to be *constantly vigilant*, because things can go wrong at the last minute.

La mona, aunque viste de seda, mona se queda.

Literal meaning: The monkey,
even if dressed in silk, is still but a monkey.

In a nutshell: Monkeys are fairly mischievous creatures. Even if you were to put them in fancy clothes, it wouldn't change their true character. This phrase is often applied to political leaders who try to change their image, but whose true colors remain unaltered.

"Los ocupantes son los mismos payasos disfrazados de ovejas, pero aunque **la mona viste de seda, mona se queda**!" Translation: "The residents are the same clowns disguised as sheep, but *we can see their true colors.*"

The**Bright** SIDE

Half empty or half full?
You decide in #35-41.

SECTION 3

alegrón de burro

Literal meaning: the donkey's big happiness

In a nutshell: When donkeys are pleased, they let out a loud cry, or bray. This call, though, only lasts about 20 seconds. For that reason, an **alegrón de burro** means "*a short-lived happiness*," usually because some expectation remains unfulfilled.

The government promised one community that had constant problems with the water supply that a public well would be drilled. When this didn't materialize, it was reported: "En la zona aparentemente se mejorarían las cosas con la construcción de un pozo, que permitiría abastecer de agua a las familias, pero todo fue un ˋ**alegrón de burro**.'" Translation: "Things apparently were to improve in the area with the construction of a well that would provide water for local families, but it turned out that *their initial happiness was short-lived*."

Algo es algo dijo el calvo, cuando le salió un pelito.

Literal meaning: Something is something, said the bald man, when a hair suddenly sprouted up.

In a nutshell: Pity the poor bald guy! How proud he is of those two or three scraggly tufts that still remain. He thinks to himself: "Thank God I'm not totally bald!" So this is akin to saying: "*Something is better than nothing.*"

The director of a governmental disaster prevention agency lamented how little he and his men were able to accomplish. "Yo sé que hay doscientos y pico de asentamientos, pero **algo es algo dijo el calvo, cuando le salió un pelito**." Translation: "I know that there are more than two hundred squatters' settlements, but *something is better than nothing.*"

37

37

A falta de pan, buenas son semitas.

Literal meaning: If there's no bread, pastries are good.

In a nutshell: A **semita** is a local pastry. So, if there's no bread around, this would be Option #2. The basic idea is: "*Something is better than nothing*." (See also **"Si no está su mamá, se conforma con su abuela**," page 42.)

OUR DAILY BREAD

Nicaraguan pastries generally are not as sweet as their Western counterparts, but when fresh, are tasty nonetheless. In a typical bakery you will find **picos**, which are triangular and basted internally with cinnamon and sometimes bits of cheese. A **polvorón**, on the other hand, is a ginger bread cookie. **Maletas** are usually filled with either meat or cheese, while **bollos** are rolls.

a precio de huate mojado

Literal meaning: for the price
of wet corn stalks

In a nutshell: For all you bargain hunters out
there, this expression should bring a smile to
your face. The corn plant is called a **huate**. If
it produces no corn and dries up, then gets
wet, it is practically worthless. If someone
is selling you something **a precio de huate
mojado**, they are giving it to you at
a bargain basement price.

"Mira mi nuevo radio. Me lo dieron **a precio
de huate mojado**." Translation: "Check out
my new radio. I got it *dirt cheap*."

como agua de mayo

Literal meaning: like May showers

In a nutshell: The greater part of Nicaragua has but two seasons: summer and winter. In reality, this is more like dry season and rainy season. Generally, the former runs from November to April, and the latter, from May to October. So by the time May rolls around, the country is one big, brown dust bowl. When those first showers fall, there is jubilation! So if something comes **como agua de mayo**, it comes "*as a blessing, as something yearned for.*"

"Justo cuando perdí mi empleo, mi tío me mandó cien dólares. Vino **como agua de mayo**." Translation: "Just when I lost my job, my uncle sent me a hundred dollars. It came *like a blessing at the right time.*"

40

Más se perdió en la guerra.

Literal meaning: More was lost in the war.

In a nutshell: During the 1980s Nicaragua was a war zone and thousands lost their lives in a terrifying civil war. So they can definitely identify with the kinds of losses that accompany warfare. If someone accidentally spills a plate of food or breaks some item around the home, someone may respond:
"**Más se perdió en la guerra**."
They are basically saying:
"*Don't worry about it.*"
It is similar to
"*Don't cry over spilt milk.*"

Si no está su mamá, se conforma con su abuela.

Literal meaning: If your mom is not around, grandma will have to do.

In a nutshell: Sadly, many children in the country are not raised by their parents, but rather, by some relative, often the grandmother. So this means "*to make do*" or "*to do the best you can with what you have.*" A similar expression is "**sacar de tripas, corazones,**" that is, "*to make hearts out of intestines.*" If you can do that, you'll really talented!

A ROCKIN' GRANDMA

If you drive by a furniture store and mention you are looking for an **abuelita**, you won't get a grandma to go. Rather, a certain kind of large rocking chairs are known by this matriarchal term.

Of A Cry Complaint

**Upset? Angry?
Express your
frustrations
in #42-55.**

arrecho

*angry, elegant, or difficult,
depending on the context*

A local coffee company has the slogan: "Café Toro:
arrecho por rendidor." Translation: "Café Toro:
lasts *like a trooper!*" Here it takes on the sense of
being valiant and bold. In contrast: "Pedro está
arrecho." Translation: "Pedro is *angry*."

bochinche

an argument or dispute

"A las dos de la madrugada se armó un tremendo
bochinche frente a la casa." Translation: "At two in
the morning there was a huge *argument* in front of
our house." Someone who is difficult to deal with
can be described as **bochinchero** or **pleitista**.

botar la gorra

Literal meaning: to throw down your hat

In a nutshell: Though soccer's popularity is growing, baseball is still considered by many to be the national sport. In the heat of the competition, a disgruntled player may throw his baseball cap to the ground in protest. So **botar la gorra** has come to signify "*to lose your cool, to get angry.*" "Cuando su jefe le dio una broma, Carlos **botó la gorra**." Translation: "When his boss played a practical joke on him, Carlos *got really mad.*"

chimirringo

very small

"¿Por qué es tan **chimirringo** este pan?" Translation: "Why is this bread so *tiny*?"

chicuije

(pronounced chee-KWEE-hay)

the smell of fish

"¡Guácala! ¿Qué es ese **chicuije**?" Translation: "Oh my God! What is that *terrible fish smell?*"

Another term for your olfactory senses is **tufo**, which means a "*bad smell*" or "*whiff*" of something. "De dónde viene ese **tufo**?" Translation: "Where is that *bad smell* coming from?"

El que no llora, no mama.

Literal meaning: He who doesn't cry, doesn't breastfeed.

In a nutshell: This is the equivalent of "*the squeaky wheel gets the grease*." Unfortunately, customer service in Nicaragua isn't the greatest. So to actually get what you want, sometimes you have to 'cry' quite a bit. A friend of mine went into a restaurant one day and saw that there was a good deal on shrimp –just 70 córdobas! But when the bill came, the waiter wanted to charge him C$100. When he complained, the fellow contested: "Sorry, but those menus are old!" So much for the customer being king! Even so, my friend kept crying until he was charged for the menu price.

¡Ideay!

(pronounced ee-EYE, the "d"
is often mute)

Literal meaning: And from there!

In a nutshell: This is the typical cry of complaint. When I first heard it, I thought it was some kind of a grunt or onomato-poeia. If someone is trying to sell you an item at an exorbitant price (which happens often, since some Nicaraguans assume that all foreigners are rich), you could say: "**¡Ideay!** Me quiere meter el batazo." That's akin to saying: "*Hey! What are you trying to do? Gouge me?*"

No hay otro palo en que ahorcarse.

Literal meaning: There is no other tree to hang yourself on.

In a nutshell: Though a most morbid thought, imagine the plight of the poor fellow who wishes to hang himself and is chagrined to discover that there is only one measly short tree around. There, with great difficulty, he carries out his macabre deed. The saying is but a crude way to say: "*There are no other possibilities.*" A shorter version of this is "**No hay de otra**." (See also "**Si no está su mamá, se conforma con su abuela,**" page 42.)

Ni picha, ni cacha, ni deja batear.

Literal meaning: [He] doesn't let you pitch, or catch, and doesn't even let you bat.

In a nutshell: Let's see. On a baseball team, what can you do? There's always a pitcher, a catcher, and many batters. But what if a person doesn't want do any of these things? Then, he *doesn't contribute anything to the team.* That's the main idea behind this beautiful baseball analogy that has made its way into the vernacular lexicon.

"Despidieron a Pedro, porque **ni picha, ni cacha, ni deja batear**." Translation: "They fired Pedro, because *he didn't contribute in the least.*"

No puedes poner a un indio a repartir chicha.

Literal translation: You can't put an Indian in charge of handing out fermented corn drink.

In a nutshell: Chicha is a common drink enjoyed even by the poor. If at a social gathering, an Indian, considered traditionally to be uneducated, is put in charge of handing it out, he may become arrogant due to his newfound "authority." As a result, he may begin to mistreat the guests. When someone who assumes a new position starts to browbeat his underlings, this saying enters into effect.

No sos ni chicha ni limonada.

Literal meaning: You are neither a fermented corn drink nor a lemonade. (Doesn't exactly roll off the tongue in English!)

In a nutshell: Chicha and lemonade are at the opposite ends of the taste spectrum. So if a person is neither one nor the other, it means that he is *riding the fence* and is *indecisive*. A political candidate who is trying to be all things to all people could have this saying applied to him.

pencazo
a large quanity
"Cayó un **pencazo** de agua."
"A *ton* of rain fell."

Quedó como la novia de Tola.

Literal meaning: She ended up like the bride from Tola.

In a nutshell: Tola is a town in southern Nicaragua, in the Department of Rivas. As the story goes, a bride there was at the altar ready to wed, but the groom never arrived. So to be left like **la novia de Tola** is to be left *hanging*. It is synonymous with the Spanish expression "**dejar plantado**."

"Iba a almorzar con Raquel, pero quedé espere y espere, y nada. **Quedé como la novia de Tola**." Translation: "I was going to have lunch with Raquel, but I was waiting and waiting, and she never showed. *She left me high and dry*."

vaina

a seed pod

In a nutshell: A **vaina** is a problem.
"**¡Qué vaina!**" is like saying "*How
terrible!*" The word **clavo** is used in similar fashion. "¡En qué clase de **clavo**
te metiste!" Translation? "Boy, you really
got yourself in a *big mess*!"

THE "MARRIAGE" TREE

The flamboyant tree or Royal Poinciana in Nicaragua is
known as the **malinche.** This botanical beauty puts on
a spectacular flower show once a year, when it blazes
to life with its intense, deep orange or yellow flowers.
Some sarcastically call it the "marriage tree." Why?
Because it flowers so infrequently and the rest of the
time looks rather forlorn and even leafless. What is
most visible are its **vainas,** or seed pods. This, too,
has a double meaning, because, as we just learned,
vainas mean "problems." So the new bride can ex-
pect her flowers once a year, and the rest of the time
is left with the lousy **vainas.**

Livin' La Vida LOCA

**There's always a party!
And things can get crazy!
Numbers 56-69 lead the way.**

SECTION 5

a la zumba marumba

Literal meaning: unknown

In a nutshell: To do something **a la zumba marumba** means to do it *"recklessly, in wild fashion,"* or *"to do a poor-quality job."* Example: "Los diputados comenzaron a entregar los fondos **a la zumba marumba**." English? "The congressmen began to hand out funds *in wild abandon*."

agarrar movido

Literal meaning: to grab [someone] moved

In a nutshell: This means *"to surprise, to catch off guard."* Reporting on a soccer game, a local newspaper observed: "**Agarraron movido** al portero." Translation: "They caught the goalie *off guard*."

andar como papalote sin cola

Literal meaning: to fly like a tail-less butterfly

In a nutshell: The long, slender tails of certain butterflies give them stability in flight. Without them, they would just go in circles. This saying, then, means "*to be disoriented, to go in circles.*" (See also "**andar como perro en procesión**," page 58.) Secondary meanings of **papalote** include "*fan*" (of the air blowing variety) and "*kite.*"

"Desde que comenzó a prepararse para la boda, Andrea **anda como papalote sin cola**." Translation: "Since she began preparing for the wedding, Andrea is *walking around like a chicken with its head cut off.*"

andar como perro en procesión

Literal meaning: to walk like a dog in procession

In a nutshell: Whether for a funeral or some religious festival, processions are common in Nicaragua. And, invariably, mingled amongst the marching hordes there is a happy dog or two. Of course, these canine party crashers have no idea what the celebration is all about. They're just along for the excitement. For that reason, **andar como perro en procesión** means "*to be completely lost, following the crowd without any rhyme or reason.*"

"Ese periodista **anda más perdido que un perro en procesión.**" Translation: "That journalist is *more lost than a dumb boy in calculus class.*"

andar de Herodes a Pilato

Literal meaning: to go from Herod to Pilate

In a nutshell: When Jesus was in his last days on earth and was being condemned by his enemies, no one really wanted to take responsibility for his death. So he was sent from Herod to Pilate. These days in Nicaragua whenever you have to do a **trámite**, that is, *paperwork*, for any kind of legal document, such as a driver's license, you will learn quickly what **andar de Herodes a Pilato** means, because you will have to go from one place to another (the bank, the Red Cross, the police station, etc.) trying to gather all the required documents.

One worker complained: "Hemos **andado de Herodes a Pilato,** de la Ceca a la Meca y no se nos ha pagado." Translation: "We had *to run all over the place* and still we haven't been paid." As you may have noticed in this quote, a synonymous expression is **andar de la Ceca a la Meca**. (See also "**pegar carrera**," page 157.)

59

andar por las cuajadas

Literal meaning: to go
by way of the cheeses

In a nutshell: This means "*to get lost, or
to be way off in one's estimations.*" Comparable to "*being out in left field.*" Similar
expressions are **andar por los ayotes** and
andar por los aguacates. These give the
basic idea of being out in the "*pumpkin
patch*" or the "*avocado fields,*" respectively.

"Al darse cuenta que estaba completamente perdido, Felipe le dijo a su esposa:
'Creo que **andamos por las cuajadas**.'"
Translation: "Realizing that he was completely lost, Felipe said to his wife: 'I think
we've made it to Timbuktu.'"

bacanal

a wild party

One newspaper headline read: "El **bacanal** lo delató. Joven denunciado por robo de 38 mil córdobas se autoinculpó al embriagarse y gastar 19 mil córdobas en alcohol en una barrera de toros." Translation: "The *wild party* gave him away. Young man accused of stealing 38,000 córdobas incriminates himself by spending 19,000 córdobas in alcohol during a rodeo." Wow! Watch out for those **bacanales**!

fuera de base

Literal meaning: off base

In a nutshell: In baseball, if a distracted runner is off base, he can be thrown out. So, metaphorically, he who is **fuera de base** is *clueless*. "Su pregunta me agarró **fuera de base**." Translation: "Your question caught me *off guard*." (See also "**agarrar movido**," page 56.)

chacuatol

*a complete mess, especially when several
items or a variety of activities
get all mixed together*

One newspaper reporting on a local horse
carriage race said the following: "Lo que
se anunció que sería uno de los espec-
táculos más grandes y llamativos del año,
fue más bien un tremendo **chacuatol**
que tuvo como resultado el desperdicio
de buenas ideas y dinero, por supuesto."
Translation: "What had been billed as one
of the biggest events of the year, turned
out instead to be *a complete mess*, and as a
result was a waste of time and money."

chimbomba

balloon

This is quite a variation from the standard Spanish "globo." "El chavalo se asustó cuando se le reventó la **chimbomba**." Translation: "The boy was startled when his *balloon* popped." Similarly, **chicle de chimbomba** is "*bubble gum.*"

paracaidista

Literal meaning: parachutist

In a nutshell: Since it's hard for the parachutist to control where he lands, a **paracaidista** is a "*party-crasher.*"

"No entablé amistad con él hasta 1968 cuando caí como **paracaidista** en una mesa donde el poeta bebía." Translation: "I didn't strike up a friendship with him until 1968, when I *uninvitedly* joined a table where the poet was drinking."

En río revuelto, ganancia de pescadores.

Literal meaning: In turbulent waters, fisherman's advantage.

In a nutshell: When the waters become turbulent, pity the poor fish! They are just looking to survive and may be momentarily disoriented. And that's to the fisherman's advantage. This adage, then, emphasizes how people take advantage of chaotic situations to their own benefit, such as those who charge exorbitant prices for ordinary goods after a natural disaster.

One man observed: "La no aplicación de procedimientos no es falta de ignorancia ni de conocimientos, es adrede. **En río revuelto, ganancia de pescadores**." Translation: "The fact that procedures are not being enforced is not due to ignorance or a lack of knowledge. It is being done on purpose. *When the cat's away, the mice will play.*"

64

samotana

*a ruckus or commotion, often because
some illegal action has taken place*

"El niño lloraba desesperado al verse en ese estado y por el estallido continuo de cohetes y la **samotana** de la multitud." Translation: "The child cried in despair because of the state he was in and because of the constant blaring of the bottle rockets and the *commotion* of the crowds."

sangoloteo

action of being thrown hither and thither

Many bus routes traverse unpaved roads. If you ask a jaded traveler just getting off the bus how his trip was, he might respond: "¡Qué clase de **sangoloteo**!" Translation: "[That stinking bus] was *throwing us all over the place.*"

The **Dark** SIDE

**Crime, corruption, hypocrisy.
Who needs to watch the movies?
There's plenty in real life!
Check it out in #70-88.**

70

¡Qué bandido!

Literal meaning: What a bandit!

In a nutshell: A **bandido** is a *bandit*, or *thief*. Figuratively, though, it can be mean *"to be cunning or deceitful."*

"¡Qué **bandido** es este Juan." Translation: "This Juan is *quite a character*!" The implied meaning may be: "*Watch out for Juan!*". The noun form is **bandidencia**, which means "*a prank, a stupid remark, or action.*"

"'Es una **bandidencia** que me quieran meter en eso', dijo Morales, quien ratificó su opinión de que se debe investigar a fondo el asunto." Translation: "'It's a *travesty* that they want to get me involved in this,' said Morales, who ratified his opinion that the matter should be thoroughly investigated.'"

Candil de la calle, oscuridad de la casa.

Literal meaning: Lamp of the street, darkness of the house.

In a nutshell: The man of the house may be a luminary in the community, and yet in his own home neglects or mistreats his family.

The headline of a recent article about Hugo Chávez, the Venezuelan President, read: "Viene Chávez: '**Candil de la calle, oscuridad de la casa**'. Llega cargado de millonarias promesas, pero en su país la pobreza crece." Translation: "Chávez is coming: He's *the bright light of the street, but the darkness of his own home*. He comes loaded with multi-million dollar promises, but in his own country poverty continues to grow."

correr al ruido de los caites

Literal meaning: running at the sound of the sandals [hitting the ground, or pavement].

In a nutshell: The **caites** are very simple *leather sandals* worn by the poor. These days they are mostly seen in traditional dances. During the 1980s on occasion this primitive footwear was even made from recycled tires. So someone running in **caites** doesn't really make that much noise at all. Whoever, then, would take off running at their sound would be the biggest of cowards. It means "*to flee at the least of provocations.*"

SANDALS WITH AN ATTITUDE

Some Nicaraguans who have lived in the United States return to their homeland, but with an attitude of superiority. The locals call them **gringos caitudos**, which means "the sandal-wearing Gringos." The idea is that, regardless of where they've been, they shouldn't forget where they came from.

en lo fino

Literal meaning: in what is delicate

In a nutshell: How would you feel if you were walking on thin ice? You would proceed with utmost caution, because the ice could break at any moment. For that reason, this idiom locally means "*to be at a crucial juncture or decisive moment.*"

One headline read: "Robo de ganado sigue **en lo fino**." Translation: "Cattle theft continues *in critical state.*"

darle sopa de muñeca

Literal meaning: to give out wrist soup

In a nutshell: This is the kind of soup you never will want to eat! Why not? Because it is a euphemism for violence, usually of the domestic variety. It's like getting a *"knuckle sandwich."* Ouch!

"Cuando su esposo está bolo, **le da sopa de muñeca.**" Translation: "When her husband gets drunk, he *gives her a knuckle sandwich.*"

estar chicle

Literal meaning: to be
a piece of chewing gum

In a nutshell: Chewing gum, though stimulating when you first put it into your mouth, soon loses its flavor and goes insipid. It is spit out as something worthless, never to be used again. So when someone makes the declaration "**Estoy chicle**," they mean "*I'm fried*" or "*I'm messed up.*"

estar hecho leña

Literal meaning: to be made firewood

In a nutshell: In Nicaragua firewood is cut one ax-stroke at a time. You are not going to be able to build any fine furniture with the splintered mess that is left over. So to be **hecho leña** means to be *"exhausted"* or *"demoralized."*

Another similar expression is to be **hecho paste**. The **paste** is the sinewy leftover of a local fruit that is used as a skin exfoliator. Many Nicaraguans have **pastes** in their showers and use them to scrub their bodies with soap. Since the **paste** is just a skeleton of its former self, the phrase **hecho paste** gives the idea of being *completely worn out*, down to the bones.

Gallina que come huevo, ni que le queman el pico.

Literal meaning: Hen that eats egg, even if you burn its beak.

In a nutshell: A hen that eats eggs? What a cannibal! If any chicken were to do that, it would be most disgusting! How would a person make that kind of beast change its ways? The idea here, then, is that "*old habits die hard.*"

"Habría que investigarlos para ver si no siguen en el tráfico de drogas, porque **gallina que come huevo ni que le quemen el pico**." Translation: "They would have to investigate to determine if they continue to traffic drugs, because *old habits die hard.*"

Another variation substitutes a dog for a hen. **"Perro que come huevo, ni que le queman el pico."**

Gato no come gato.

Literal meaning: Cat doesn't eat cat.

In a nutshell: Cats don't eat other cats. Everyone knows that. The idea here is that people who are from the same organization, or who are on the same level economically or otherwise should not try to dominate one another. Thieves, for example, don't steal from other thieves. An article about a truce between two political parties had this saying as a headline.

A CAT WITH BEAUTIFUL EYES: YOU!

Don't be surprised if you hear someone describing you to a third party with these words: "¿Ya conoces a la fulana? Ella es alta, delgadita, y es **gata**." Literal meaning: "Do you know So and So? She's tall, kind of slender, and she's a *cat*." Now don't get your whiskers ruffled! And watch those claws, I mean, nails! Your friend is merely saying that you have *green or blue* eyes. Since the majority of Nicaraguans have brown eyes, besides foreigners the main possessors of those colored eyes are our feline friends.

Las cosas no son del dueño, sino del que las necesita.

Literal meaning: Things don't belong to the owner, but rather to the one who needs them.

In a nutshell: Sadly, today the line between what is mine and what is yours has been blurred. Although Nicaragua is still the safest country in Central America, petty theft is rampant. Such crooks are known locally as **amigos de lo ajeno**, that is, *"friends of what belongs to others."* (See also "**When a tamale goes bad**," page 118.)

huaca

(pronounced WAH-kah)

A hidden, generally illicit treasure, a stash.

Back in 2002 a huge scandal broke out surrounding former President Arnoldo Alemán, who allegedly had pilfered millions of dollars during his term as president. The scandal was known throughout the country as "**La Huaca**" or "The *Great Stash*."

"¿Ya hallaste los riales? ¿Dónde estaba la **huaca**?" Translation: "Did you find the money? Where was the *stash*?"

hacérsele el cambiolín

Literal meaning: to do the switcheroo on someone

In a nutshell: The verb "cambiar" means "*to change*," but this expression means "*to pull a switcheroo*," always in a fraudulent way. Con artists deceive the unwary by promising one thing and giving another.

One newspaper article described how two men in a taxi promised one woman to take her to some money changers with whom they were in collusion. It turns out that they were using counterfeit bills and others that, because they are no longer is circulation, are worthless. The headline read: "Sujetos le querían '**hacer el cambiolín**.'" Translation: "Subjects tried '*to pull the switcheroo*' on her."

BUYER BEWARE!

Other terms that have similar meaning are **dar gato por liebre**, which applies especially if what you received isn't what you ordered. (It literally means "*to give cat instead of a hare.*") **Dar vuelta** also transmits the idea of being swindled. Watch your wallet!

---

maña

a trick to get something to work

For example, perhaps you're fiddling with a key, trying unsuccessfully to open a gate. Someone comes and says: "Dejámelo a mí. Te voy a mostrar una **maña**." Translation: "Here, let me try. I'm going to show you a *trick*." And it opens right up! On the other hand, if someone is said to be **mañoso**, it means he has probably learned too many tricks for his own good. He is likely a *shady character*.

perro zompopo

Literal meaning: ant dog

In a nutshell: The **perro zompopo** is no dog at all, but refers to small lizards that are seen everywhere. These little guys let out a clicking noise that sounds almost like a bark. You are likely to see them even indoors. But don't worry! They don't bite and seem to do more good than harm.

piñatear

to take public assets as one's own

Daniel Ortega is locally lambasted as "**El Piñatín**" for his role in freely giving away state goods to his party members.

"La Alcaldía de Managua tiene potestad para confiscar o **piñatear** propiedades privadas para la construcción del nuevo Hospital Militar." Translation: "Managua City Hall has the power invested in it to *confiscate* private properties so as to build the new Military Hospital."

poncharse

Literal meaning: to be punched

In a nutshell: This is yet another term popularized through baseball. In that sport it means "*to strike out.*"

"Freddy **se ponchó**." Translation: "Freddy *struck out*."

Figuratively, it means "*to fail.*" "Chepito se fue a buscar trabajo todo el día, pero **se ponchó**." Translation: "Chepito was looking for work all day long, but he *failed*."

In another context, the adjective **ponchado** can mean "*punctured*." A **llanta ponchada** is a "*flat tire*." (See "**If your car breaks down...**", Page 171.)

por debajera

Literal meaning: On the undersides

In a nutshell: This means "*behind the scenes*," and has a negative connotation, which is used frequently in political circles.

"A Hilario le estaban pagando **por debajera**." Translation: "They were paying Hilario *under the table*."

Unos a la bulla, y otros a la cabulla.

Literal meaning: Some go to the noise, and others go to the rope.

In a nutshell: For Nicaraguans noise is a most desirable thing. Some of their traditions involve parading through the streets with marching bands sometimes at five or six in the morning! And on holidays you will hear firecrackers go off until you are tone deaf. So the reference to **bulla** alludes to noisy traditional festivals or other special occasions. In rural areas, it would be common to go to such events on a horse.

The **cabulla**, on the other hand, is a natural fiber rope. Unfortunately, with everyone distracted by the party, it was a good opportunity for thieves to carry out their evil plans. They would use the **cabulla** to steal cattle and other animals. So the saying highlights how people can be *opportunistic for perverse ends.* (See also "**En río revuelto, ganancia de pescadores**," page 64.)

zafarse

to come undone, or to get away

"Mientras caminaba por la pasarela, *se le zafó* el zapato." Translation: "While she was walking down the runway, her shoe *fell off*."

All in the Family

Where there's a will,
there's a relative! Get
all warm and fuzzy
with #89-98.

SECTION 7

chavalo

a boy, or a guy

"Ese **chavalo** ya está en sexto grado."
Translation: "That *boy* is already in sixth
grade." The diminutive, "**chavalitos**,"
takes on the sense of "*little kids*."

cumiche

the baby, or youngest child, of the family

This word derives from Nahuatl roots which mean "little skirt." Centuries ago before the advent of modern clothing, each child wore a skirt, and the baby of the family of course had the smallest skirt of all, and hence the term.

"Enrique es el **cumiche** de la familia." Translation: "Enrique is the *baby* of the family." Another interesting local word involving family relationships is **entenado**, which means "stepson."

chinear

to hold (a child)

A mother might say to her small child: "Querés que te **chinee**?" Translation: "Do you want me *to hold* you?"

On the other hand, when people hold their child excessively, they are spoiling them. That is why the intensified form **chinchinear** means "*to dote, or spoil with affection.*"

"Las abuelas siempre andan **chinchineando** a sus nietos." Translation: "Grandmothers are always *spoiling* their grandchildren."

chirizo

straight hair that stands on end

Usually only men are described as **chirizo,** because the hair has to be short enough that it will not lay flat. Many men in the Masaya area who are of indigenous extraction have this type of hair.

Person A: "¿Cómo es él?"
Person B: "Es bajito y **chirizo**."

Translation: "What's he like?"
"He's short and *has straight hair that stands on end*."

Hijo del tigre nace rayado.

Literal meaning: The son of a tiger
is born with stripes.

In a nutshell: A tiger has no choice but to
be born with stripes; it's in the DNA. So, too,
children tend to inherit their parents' talents.
This is the equivalent of "*the apple doesn't fall
far from the tree*" or a "*chip off the old block.*"

An article about children that follow in their
parents' footsteps had this introduction: "Un
viejo refrán dice: **hijo de tigre nace rayado**.
Eso es precisamente lo que ocurrió con estos
tres chavalos, quienes siguen hoy en día el
ejemplo de vida que les dio su padre." Translation: "An old saying states: '*The apple doesn't
fall far from the tree.*' That is precisely what
happened with these three boys, who today
follow their father's example."

jaña

girlfriend

One creative writer speaking of what a person could do with a pair of expensive tennis shoes, suggested: "Cuando están lavaditas, bien podés visitar a tu **jaña**, sacarla a pasear, ir a bacanalear, llevarla a cine, e ir a comer pizza." Translation: "When they are nice and washed, you might as well visit your *girlfriend*, take her out for a spin, go to wild parties, take her to the movies, and go eat pizza." (See also **"The Big Pull**," page 96.)

FANCY A SLICE OF PEEK-SAH?

For some reason, many Nicaraguans have a strange way of pronouncing the word **pizza**. Instead of PEET-sah, they say PEEK-sah, as if there were some mid-word k. The same thing happens with the word for "swimming pool," **piscina**, which many pronounce as PEEK-see-nah. And if you don't want a Coca-Cola, you'll have to order a **Pepsi**, that is, a "PECK-see." Hmm, by the way, would you mind if I had a slice of that, uh, peeksa?

juntos, pero no revueltos

Literal meaning: Together, but not scrambled

In a nutshell: Poverty has obligated many families to live together. When the kids grow up and get married, instead of getting their own place, they build a small room on the family's property. I knew one extended family who came to number 55 souls! In these conditions, even though they are living "together," they don't want to be "scrambled" by getting involved in each other's personal affairs.

If you could ask someone what it's like to live surrounded by so many people, they might respond: "Vivimos **juntos, pero no revueltos**." Translation: "We live *together, but each of us still has his personal space.*"

lampazo

a mop

It also occurs in verb form, **lampacear**. "Juanita, ¿cuándo vas a **lampacear** la casa?" Translation: "Juanita, when are you going *to mop* the house?"

pacha

a baby bottle

"Dále a tu hermanito su **pacha**." Translation: "Give your little brother his *bottle*."

pipe

(pronounced PEE-pay)

a small child

By extension, if someone is said to be **pipes** with someone else, it means they are *close friends*. When two people of the opposite sex are first beginning to spend a lot of time together, observers will likely describe their **pipencia**, or *closeness*. Other words used to describe small children are **cipotes**, **chigüines** (pronounced chee-WEEN-es), and **chavalitos**.

THE BIG PULL

Don't be shocked if you hear someone say: "Mi hijo ya está **jalando**." This literally means: "My son is *pulling*." But this is a metaphorical pull, as **jalar** is the local term for "*dating*." And I'm not pulling your leg! It is also sometimes written as **halar**. Many businesses have this word written on their entrance doors to mean "pull," or "open."

Food
FOR THOUGHT

**Hungry yet? Numbers
99-131 are sure to make
your mouth water!**

Barriga llena, corazón contento.

Literal translation: Full tummy, happy heart.

In a nutshell: How we love to eat! This expression verbalizes one's contentment after a fine meal. (See also "**Indio comido puesto al camino,**" page 107.)

buñuelos

a dessert consisting of fried yucca donut holes served with syrup

caballo bayo

Literal meaning: horse horse

an assortment of meats, usually grilled

In a nutshell: There's no horse meat included in this succulent pantry of grilled meats. "Mi abuelita nos invitó a un **caballo bayo**." Translation: "My grandma invited us to a *grilled meat smorgasbord*."

NO HORSING AROUND

To call someone a **caballo** is like saying "*You idiot!*". In English, we sometimes say that someone is as strong as a horse, but this is best not translated literally, because your listener will think you are saying he works like an idiot. A **caballada** is any foolish move or action. If a reckless driver cuts you off in traffic, you might shriek: "¡Qué **caballada**!" Translation: "*What an idiotic move!*" A foolish person can also be called a **bayunco**.

chingaste

sediment in typical drinks

In a nutshell: If you have learned Spanish elsewhere, you might be a bit put off by this term. But relax! There's nothing vulgar about **chingaste**. (Say it out loud 10 times to get it out of your system!)

When you are finished drinking one of Nicaragua's popular drinks, such as **pinollillo**, **cacao**, or **avena**, you will notice that a lot of the material used to make the drink has formed a sediment at the bottom of your glass. And all that stuff left over in the bottom of your glass is called **chingaste**.

"¿No te vas a comer el **chingaste**?" Translation: "Aren't you going to eat *the sediment from your drink*?" Yummy!

chancho

pig

While other Latin American countries use words like "puerco" or "marrano," this is the local word for "*pig*."

"¿En cuánto vende ese **chancho**?" Translation: "How much are you selling that *pig* for?"

WHAT A PIGSTY!

The poor pig has such a nasty reputation. A **chancha-da** is a "*dirty act*" or a "*mess*." A mother may enter her son's room and shout: "Chavalo, ¡limpiáme esta **chanchada** ahorita!" Translation: "Boy, you had better clean up this *pigsty* right now!" If you ever have need to shoo a pig, shout out a hearty "**¡Cuche!**"

cosa de horno

baked goods made of corn

One popular type of baked goods are
rosquillas, which usually come in cookie-
size circles. "El Viejo es famoso por sus
rosquillas." Translation: "The town of El
Viejo [near Chinandega] is famous for its
typical corn pastries."

cusuco

armadillo

Hold on to your stomach! In rural
Nicaragua this animal is still hunted and
eaten! So make sure you know
what's in that hamburger!

chompipe

turkey

While most of Latin America uses the generic "pavo," and the Mexicans have their "guajolote," the Nicaraguans gobble up their **chompipe**, yet another word derived from Nahuatl.

WHAT'S IN A NAME?

You will likely catch on quickly to the local custom of giving people often unflattering nicknames behind their backs. One fellow I knew had a double chin that wouldn't quit. He was known in the entire town simply as **Chompipe**. So, before coming to Nicaragua, you might want to hit that gym again! Otherwise, you never know what you might be called. Gobble, gobble! (See "**Lo que no mata, engorda**," page 109.)

gallo pinto

fried rice and beans

Gallo pinto literally means "the spotted rooster," but this colorful term is chicken-less. Though it's tasty enough, most foreigners are astonished at its frequency —it's regularly eaten for breakfast and for dinner several times during the week. One comic once quipped: "I'm not afraid of the bullet; it's the *velocity* that scares me." I say the same about **gallo pinto**. I am not afraid of it. But its *frequency* is what scares me!

FAST FOOD ON A BUDGET

Gallo pinto is one of the offerings at the local **fritangas**. These family-run businesses are Nicaragua's answer to fast food. Besides the ubiquitous rice and beans dish, you will likely find the following: **carne asada**, *grilled beef*; **pollo asado**, *grilled chicken*; **chancho asado** *grilled pork*; **maduro,** *ripe fried plaintains*; **tajadas,** *green plaintains cut like potato chips and fried*; and **queso frito,** *fried cheese*. Many places will wrap it up in a banana leaf —talk about biodegradable packaging! For the equivalent of two or three US dollars, you'll be stuffed!

guaro

liquor

"Ese picado solo anda con su **guaro**."
Translation: "That drunk is always walking around with his *booze*."

güirila

(pronounced wee-REE-lah)

type of tortilla made from new corn

huevos de amor

Literal meaning: love eggs

*chicken eggs that have been fertilized natu-
rally, as opposed to commercially
purchased ones*

indio viejo

Literal meaning: old Indian

*a typical dish made of corn,
meat, and spices.*

Don't worry. It's probably
no one you know!

Indio comido puesto al camino.

Literal meaning: The Indian who has finished eating is on his way.

In a nutshell: The English equivalent of "*eat and run.*" The satisfied visitor, having just finished his meal, typically offers this justification for not sticking around. So if you are offered a meal, say this graciously to your host just before you say your goodbyes.

ONE LITTLE, TWO LITTLE, THREE LITTLE INDIANS...

The next time you hear term #112, shock your hosts by responding: "**Indio sentado, espera otro bocado**." That means: "*The seated Indian awaits another bite.*" Or if someone invited to the meal doesn't show up, say: "**Un indio menos, un bocado más**." This literally conveys the idea: "*One Indian less, one more mouthful.*" The idea? "Then there's more for us!" Yet another variation is "**Un indio menos, un plátano más**." That means "*One Indian less, one more plantain.*"

jocote

a small, round fruit

This member of the cashew family is pictured on the cover of this book. In the León area, try **cusnaca**, a typical dish of baked **jocotes**.

machigüe

(pronounced mah-CHEE-gway)

*daily scraps mixed together
and given to the pigs*

"Echen esas sobras en el **machigüe**."
Translation: "Throw those leftovers into
the *pig slop*."

Lo que no mata, engorda.

Literal meaning: What doesn't kill you fattens you up.

In a nutshell: This is a common saying when food is being offered, especially something that you have never tried before. It's like saying: "*Well, it can't hurt.*" Not exactly a good motto for dieters.

mantenedora

Literal meaning: the thing that keeps

a large, usually horizontal cooler

If you go to the **pulpería** (see page 115) for a cold **gaseosa**, or "*soda,*" the person who waits on you will probably pull your purchase from one of these. Or you might ask for a **fresco**, a local fruit drink.

109

merol

an informal word for food

"Y, ¿de **merol**? ¿Cuál va a ser el menú?"
Translation: "And for *food*? What's the
menu going to be?" Food sometimes is
also referred to informally as **el golpe**.
When people are hungry they might say:
"Tengo que matar el **tigre**." That literally
means: "I have to kill the *tiger*." That's because when we're famished, our stomachs
send out a tiger-like growl!

mondongo

*a soup made of beef tripe, similar to the
Mexican "menudo" but without tomatoes*

nacatamal

Nacatamal (see picture, page 97) means "*meat tamale*" in Nahuatl. Drive through Managua on a Sunday morning and you will see taxis lining the streets in front of eateries ready to buy this traditional breakfast. At the center of this local delicacy is a paprika-seasoned cornmeal mixture with tasty chunks of pork and potatoes and a smattering of rice. Some of the deluxe versions will throw in a raisin or two, or perhaps an olive. Onions, green peppers, and tomatoes round out the combination together with just a smidgeon of mint. Wrapped in a banana leaf and boiled for hours, usually over an open fire, **nacatamales** have a unique, slightly bitter flavor. To eat one, just unwrap the banana leaf, and go to it!

AS ROTUND AS A CONGRESSMAN

Tell a Nicaraguan that you're going to have a **nacatamal** and he might exclaim: "¡**Nacatambuche!**" The **buche** is the *chicken's stomach*, so the term seems to suggest that eating one of these babies will definitely leave you full! (See **fulear**, page 160.) Others refer to them as **diputados**, which means "*congressmen*," who tend to be as rotund as these Sunday morning specials.

paila

a pan for cooking

"Ester tiene todas sus **pailas** colgadas en la cocina." Translation: "Ester has all her *pans* hanging in the kitchen." A large pot for cooking soup is called a **porra**.

pajilla

a drinking straw

"Pasáme una **pajilla**, por favor." Translation: "Please pass me a *straw*."

pichinga

*a 40-liter container for carrying liquids,
usually milk or other dairy products*

"Traéme la **pichinga**. Vamos a ordeñar las
vacas." Translation: "Bring me the *big milk
cylinder*. Let's go milk the cows."

pinol

a typical drink made of toasted ground corn, sugar, and cacao

The Nicaraguans are so enamored by it that they are known in Central America by their nickname **pinoleros**. If you practice and perfect the words and phrases in this book, the locals may some day give you this glowing compliment: "**¡Sos más nica que el pinol!**" That means: "*You're more Nicaraguan than pinol!*"

pozol

Our Mexican readers will be reminded of their beloved soup, "pozole." But in Nicaragua **pozol** is not a soup, but rather a drink made of cooked corn meal and usually served chilled.

pulpería

a neighborhood general store

Hungry? Thirsty? Just head to one of these family-run stores. They sell everything from crackers to toilet paper and they are everywhere!

NO OCTUPUS SERVED HERE!

Since **pulpo** means "octopus," a foreigner could easily mistake a **pulpería** for some seafood outlet. In reality, though, this is the term for the family-run shops mentioned above. Just a step up are **distribuidoras**, which usually have a bit more selection. And, you're really moving up if you can make it to a **mini-super**, just a step below the supermarket. On the other hand, a **tiangue** is a small market, sometimes with several individual stalls where merchants sell their goods.

quesillo

*a kind of cheese, served cold on a tortilla
and smothered in cream
and pickled onions*

The towns most famous for their **quesillo**
are on the road from Managua to León:
Nagarote and La Paz Centro.

raspado

Literal meaning: a scrape

*a shaved ice snow cone, which comes
in a wide variety of flavors*

rondón

*a typical Atlantic Coast stew made with meat,
fish, and turtle meat in a coconut milk base*

This word actually comes from the English term
"run down." The idea is that this will energize
you when you're feeling run down.

*Una vez al año
no hace daño.*

Literal meaning: [To do something]
once a year does no harm.

In a nutshell: Everyone knows we should watch
what we eat. But few have the self-control to re-
sist temptation. And this phrase justifies it all. It's
almost like saying *"I'll splurge just this once."*

vigorón

Getting worn out? Tired? What you need is to hop over to Granada and eat a **vigorón**! The term literally means "vim and vigor." It is a bed of cooked yucca covered with fried pork skins and drizzled in a spicy cabbage salad. The belief is that eating one of these babies will get you back up to snuff. The idea behind **rondón,** on the previous page, is quite similar.

yoltamal

a sweet tamale made with new corn

WHEN A TAMALE GOES BAD
Tamalear has become a slang term for stealing. A few years ago, former President Arnoldo Alemán was caught pilfering millions in public funds. The locals quickly dubbed him "**El Tamalón**," literally "*The Big Tamale*," that is, "*The Great Thief*." "¡Ay!, me **tamalearon** la ropa que dejé tendida." Translation: "Oh no, they *swiped* the clothes I left on the line." (See also **huaca**, page 78.)

Your Health
To

**Eat right, exercise regularly, die anyway.
Read all about it in #132-137.**

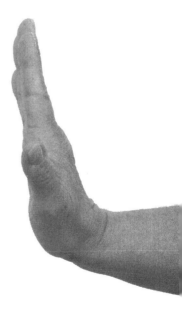

canilla

the leg, or shin

"Me sacaron sin pastillas porque no hay, me siento todo mareado y me duele mi **canilla**."

Translation: "They released me [from the hospital] without giving me any pills because there aren't any. I feel dizzy and my *leg* hurts."

El que peca y reza empata.

Literal translation: He who sins and prays, ties.

In a nutshell: In Nicaragua's Catholic tradition the man who sins has an easy solution for forgiveness: he goes to the priest and confesses. He'll get prescribed a few Hail Marys, and Bob's your uncle! (See "**Muerta la lora y que nadie la llore**," page 175.) Of course, this doesn't change his conduct in the least, because he always has the option of returning the following week to get atonement for his most recent charades. These days, though, the phrase has taken on the more secular meaning of being "moderate in habits."

When one man was asked about his health, he responded: "Soy, para todo en mi vida, de los que **peca y reza para empatar**, sin excesos, siempre moderado." Translation: "All my life I have been among those who believes that *over time everything evens itself out*, so I have avoided excesses and exercised moderation." In a similar vein, one blogger posted a picture of an order of McDonalds' French fries next to a can of ultra weight loss shake. The caption? **El que peca y reza, empata**.

121

colgar los tenis

Literal meaning: to hang up your tennis shoes

In a nutshell: When an athlete hangs up his tennis shoes, he is probably retiring from the sport. But this popular phrase speaks of a much more permanent retirement. It is a euphemism for death. "Panchito ya **colgó los tenis**." Translation: "Panchito *kicked the bucket*."

El que por su gusto muere, que lo entierre parado.

Literal meaning: If someone dies because of his own poor choices, let him be buried standing.

In a nutshell: A person may make poor decisions in life and hasten his own death. If such an individual, in effect, dies of his own foolishness, some may not view him worthy of an honorable burial. The basic idea, then, is that we have to face the consequences of our actions. It is similar to the saying "*You made your bed, and you have to lie in it.*"

For example, some build their homes in areas where flooding is common. Every time flood waters come, they have to be evacuated. Commenting on this, one local wrote: "La gente tiene la culpa y también la alcaldía por permitirles vivir y construir cerca de los cauces. La gente sabe bien que cuando llueve, las correntadas de agua no perdonan. A como dice el dicho '**el que por su gusto muere**...'" Translation: "The people are to blame and so is City Hall for allowing them to build and live near the drainage ditches. People well know that when it rains those strong currents are unforgiving. Like the saying goes: '*If you put yourself in harm's way...*'"

La Pelona

A friend of mine who has been ill for years told me one day: "Anoche sentí que **la Pelona** se me acercó y me quiso oler el pelo." This literally means: "Last night *the bald lady* came close to me and was trying to smell my hair." Who is this bald woman? It's nothing more than a euphemism for death. If someone says that **la Pelona** came near to them, they are suggesting their demise is imminent.

perder las llaves

Literal meaning: to lose your keys

In a nutshell: One day a co-worker came late and I asked what happened. The response was: "**Perdí las llaves**." Translation: "I *lost the keys*." At that moment I was dumbfounded. What keys? It turns out she was talking about the keys to her digestive tract —a clever euphemism for *diarrhea*.

Good Grief!

**Excited? Disgusted? Surprised?
What are you going to do about it?
Get ideas in #138-143!**

¡Chocho!

While our friends from Spain will blush at this one, there is nothing vulgar with this common interjection that means: "*Wow!*" Though its popularity has waned somewhat, in times past it was so prevalent that the Costa Ricans referred to Nicaraguans as the "**chochos**."

¡Cómo vas a creer!

Literal translation: How are you going to believe!

In a nutshell: This really means "You're kidding!" For example: "¿Escuchaste que la María está encinta? "**¡Cómo vas a creer!**" Translation: "Did you hear María is pregnant?" "*You're kidding!*"

¡Guácala!

an interjection of disgust

"**¡Guácala!** Pobre los que tienen que recoger café. ¡Cuantas culebras les habrán picado!" Translation: "*How disgusting!* The poor people who have to pick coffee, how many times they must have been bitten by snakes!"

¡Solo vos sabés!

Literal meaning: Only you know!

In a nutshell: This means: "Who knows!" This is an excellent phrase to diffuse an argument. If you feel that you're barking up the wrong tree with someone, just say with a chuckle: "**¡Solo vos sabés!**". And walk away.

¡Ni quiera Dios!

Literal meaning: May God
not want [that]!

In a nutshell: This is the
local version of "*God forbid!*".

Recently the local newspaper reported on
an attempt to introduce motorcycle taxis
(known as **caponeras**) in Managua.
One local wrote in: "**Ni quiera Dios**,
sería una invasión de esos aparatos en
nuestra ciudad, la cual está plagada de
tantos taxis." Translation: "*God forbid!*
That would mean an invasion of those
contraptions in our city, which
is plagued with so many taxis."

¡Qué bárbaro!

Literal meaning: How barbarous!

In a nutshell: You will hear this exclamation over and over again in Nicaragua. It's meaning will depend a lot on the context and runs the gamut from "*Amazing!*" to "*Awesome!*" to "*Incredible!*"

"¡**Qué bárbaro**, pensé que estábamos platicando como amigos!" Translation: "*I can't believe it!* I thought we were talking as friends!"

"Jorge acaba de pegar un cuadrangular con las bases llenas. ¡**Qué bárbaro!**" Translation: "Jorge just hit a grand slam. *Awesome!*"

Our Social Network

**Having friends is better
than having money.
See why in #144-150!**

adiós

Everyone knows **adiós** means "*goodbye.*" But in Nicaragua it sometimes means "*hello.*" When you are passing an acquaintance on the street, just say "**adiós**." It's like hello and goodbye all wrapped up in one.

Hablando del rey de Roma, y mirá quién se asoma.

Literal translation: Talking of the king of Rome, look who shows up.

In a nutshell: This is the equivalent of "*speak of the Devil.*" If you are talking about someone and at the precise moment they show up, this is the phrase to use.

chele

a person of white skin color, a foreigner

The marvelous thing about Nicaragua is that racial tensions are practically nil. People seem more divided by social and economic standing than by color.

If you are a light-skinned foreigner, you will get called this all the time. When you go into the market you will hear: "¿Qué le damos, **chelito**?" Translation: "What can we get for you, *whitey?*" Again, don't get excited about this. It is said with affection. In a similar way, if a black woman goes shopping, she will likely hear: "¿Qué le damos, **morenita**?" Translation: "What are you looking for, *blackie*?" These terms are completely inoffensive.

molote

a large crowd of people

"¿Viste ese **molote** de gente en la esquina?" Translation: "Did you see that *crowd of people* on the street?"

That reminds me of a popular understatement. For example, someone might say: "¿Viste ese **poco de gente** que llegaron?" Literally, this means, "Did you see those *few people* that arrived?" However, in Nicaragua the opposite meaning is intended. It really means: "The place was *packed*."

No es lo mismo verla venir que platicar con ella.

Literal meaning: Watching her come isn't the same as talking with her.

In a nutshell: From a distance it's easy to be enamored by a beautiful woman approaching in the distance. But how will we feel about her once we have talked up front and personal? Our viewpoint may change drastically. So this is akin to *"Don't judge a book by its cover."*

It can be applied to any kind of offer we receive. Perhaps we are presented with a job opportunity that initially seems enticing. But once we read the fine print and do some research, we may be otherwise inclined. (See also "**Otro gallo cantará**," page 16.)

sentirse como pollo comprado

Literal meaning: to feel like a purchased chicken

In a nutshell: Live chickens can be purchased at the municipal markets. So when a live chicken is purchased and brought home, immediately the other chickens come up to peck at him —not exactly a warm welcome! That's why if someone feels like a **pollo comprado**, he's feeling *out of place*, like a fish out of water, or a fifth wheel.

tener pegazón

Literal meaning: To have stickiness

In a nutshell: To be very closely attached to someone. "Los padres **tenemos esa pegazón** por los hijos y no dejamos que sean independientes." Translation: "As parents we have that *strong attachment* to our children and don't let them go out on their own." (See also "**pipencia**," page 96.)

Making The Bucks

It doesn't fall from heaven, but we can't live without it. Read the good, the bad, and the ugly in #151-161!

Alejandro en puño

Literal meaning: Alexander in fist

In a nutshell: This refers to the quintessential miser. A tight-fisted individual is unwilling to share with others. He may be said to be **tacaño** or **pinche**. This last term is informal, but not vulgar, as is the case in some Latin American countries.

"No le pida nadie a Elías. Ese **Alejando en puño** no le dará ni un chelín." Translation: "Don't ask Elías for anything. That *miser* won't give you a dime!"

Coyol quebrado, coyol comido.

Literal meaning: Coyol that is broken, coyol that is eaten.

In a nutshell: The **coyol** is a small local fruit. To eat one of them, you first have to break the skin. Since most Nicaraguans live on a limited income, they can only afford to buy the food for each day. This saying is similar to living "*hand to mouth*" in English.

coyote

Those living near the Mexico-U.S. border use this term to refer to those who lead illegal aliens into the United States. But in Nicaragua a **coyote** refers to men and some women who exchange dollars and córdobas on the streets. Of course, at one time literal **coyotes** could be found in the country. A fortress located at the entrance to Masaya is called **Coyotepe**, which means in Nahuatl "*Coyote Mountain*."

De grano en grano, se llena la gallina el gran buche.

Literal meaning: Grain by grain, the hen fills her big gizzard.

In a nutshell: Little by little, great things can be accomplished. "*By an inch, it's a cinch; by a yard, it's hard.*" A family may have difficulties making ends meet, but if they each keep saving a little bit each week, eventually they will be able to save up to buy something they want or need.

Desvistió a Juan para vestir a Pedro.

Literal translation: They undressed Juan to dress Pedro.

In a nutshell: This is the equivalent of "*robbing Peter to pay Paul*," to take away from someone to give to another. One official spoke of his efforts to distribute relief aid amongst those in diverse geographic areas. "'No queremos **desvestir a Pedro para vestir a Pablo,**' ejemplificó en alusión a que tanto la RAAN como los departamentos del Norte y el Occidente necesitan de recursos." Translation: "'*We don't want to rob Peter to pay Paul*,' for example, in allusion to the RAAN [The North Atlantic Autonomous Region] as well as the northern and western departments, which also need resources."

El que tiene más galillo, traga más pinol.

Literal meaning: He who has a bigger throat can swallow more pinol.

In a nutshell: Those who have bigger throats can gulp down more of this typical Nicaraguan ground corn drink. The idea? The rich get richer. People tend to use their resources selfishly for their own good. "Desgraciadamente estamos en un municipio donde **el que tiene mas galillo traga mas pinol.**" Translation: "Unfortunately, we are in a town where *the rich get richer* and the poor get poorer."

En arca abierta
hasta el justo peca.

Literal translation: In an open contribution box,
even the righteous one sins.

In a nutshell: Contribution boxes are generally
well locked. But what if they weren't? What if
they were completely open? In that case, it would
become a large temptation even for
an honest, or righteous person.

In an article about how government funds are
being used directly for party interests and bypassing traditional processes, one man wrote: "Esto es
para saquear la plata de los impuestos que pagan
los nicaragüenses y robársela. Pero como no hay
contralores, pues **en arca abierta, el justo peca**."
Translation: "This is to loot all the tax money
Nicaraguans are paying and steal it away.
But since there are no comptrollers,
a bad padlock invites a picklock."

Eso son otros cien pesos.

Literal meaning: That's another hundred pesos.

In a nutshell: When some foreigners have first heard this expression, they jump to grab their wallets. In reality, though, this just means "*that's a completely different story*," or "*that's a completely different matter.*"

A FOOL AND HIS MONEY...

The local currency is called the **córdoba** in honor of Francisco Hernández de Córdoba, founder of the cities of Granada and León. Money in general terms is often called **riales**, so when offering some product, a common complaint of the potential buyer is "**No hay riales**," that is, "*There's no money.*" They might also say, "**Estoy palmado.**" In colloquial speech the local bills are also called **varas**, or **golpes**. The preferred currency, of course, is the U.S. dollar, known as a **lapa**, a parrot known for its green color, or a **lolo**.

ipegüe

(pronounced ee-PEG-way)

Ever heard of the "*baker's dozen*"? The
ipegüe is essentially the same idea. The next
time you go to the market and buy a dozen
lemons or oranges, negotiate the price. Then
when they are finished packing them up, say:
"Y ¿el **ipegüe**?" Your excellent Nicaraguan
Spanish will bring a smile to the merchant's
face, and he will throw in number 13 for
free! Just with this tip, you will more than
pay for the price of this book!

jarana

a debt

"Pedro **se enjaranó** hasta el cuello." Translation: "Pedro *is in debt* up to his neck."

The adjective form is **enjaranado**. "Lo que pocos sabían más allá del ámbito familiar es que Manuel estaba **enjaranado**."
Translation: "What few people outside the family knew is that Manual was *in debt*."

Según el sapo es la pedrada.

Literal translation: The stone you throw depends on the toad.

In a nutshell: Young mischievous boys in the country have a hankering for killing every critter that moves. When they catch sight of a toad, they look for the nearest rock. But how big a rock? That depends on the size of the toad. For that reason this saying means "*to take measures that are in accord with a given situation.*"

For example, a friend of mine works for a graphic design firm in the country. I asked him how he calculates how much to charge each customer, and his response was the above-mentioned. In other words, if the client were a large company, a large toad, if you will, the charge would be more.

148

Time
FOR EVERYTHING

Procrastination is the
thief of time, so fly
through #162-172!

ahorita

This means "*right now*" and not "later" as in some other Latin countries.

"¿Puedes venir **ahorita**?" Translation: "Can you come *right now*?"

balazo

Literal meaning: a bullet shot

super fast

"Cuando Jaime oyó que había muerto su abuela, se vino **balazo** a casa." Translation: "When Jaime heard that his grandmother had died, he *came flying* home."

Cayendo el muerto, soltando el llanto.

Literal translation: As he falls dead, the crying breaks out.

In a nutshell: When a loved one dies, no one needs to tell us: "Go ahead and cry." That is something that comes immediately and without prompting. For that reason, "**Cayendo el muerto, soltando el llanto**" refers to an immediate reaction or response to any particular provocation.

"Sé que en cuanto mi esposa dé a luz, mi suegra va a estar aquí diario. **Cayendo el muerto, soltando el llanto**." Translation: "I know that when my wife gives birth, my mother-in-law is going to be here every day. It is going to be *an immediate reaction*."

This is also used when one expects immediate pay for services rendered.

contra el cacho

Literal meaning: against the horn

In a nutshell: In basic English, it means "*running late.*" You'll soon find that Nicaraguans are quite often running late. In fact, they joke about **la hora nica**, that is, Nicaraguan time. If you are invited to a social gathering that is to start at 5:30 in the afternoon and you arrive on time, you will surely be among *the first* to arrive. In fact, most of the time you will be *the only one* there. While in some business circles appointments are expected to be punctual, large social gatherings notoriously start late.

"Oíme, voy **contra el cacho**. Creo que no voy a llegar hasta las ocho." Translation: "Hey, I'm *running late*. I probably won't get there until eight."

corre corre

Literal meaning: run run

In a nutshell: This means *"hustle and bustle."*

"En el restaurante se puede apreciar el **corre corre** de los meseros ordenando las mesas como hormiguitas trabajadoras." Translation: "In the restaurant you can appreciate the *hustle and bustle* of the waiters arranging the tables like worker ants."

echar un peloncito

Literal meaning: to throw a bald guy

In a nutshell: This idiom really means "*to take a nap*." Since **pelón** is slang for "*bald*," it could have reference to the fact that older men, a good number of whom are now hairless, are most frequently seen napping.

"No molestés a tu papá. Está **echando un peloncito**." Translation: "Don't bother your father. He's *taking a nap*."

en carrera

quickly

"Me vine **en carrera**." Translation: "I came *right away*."

estar en la cola de un venado

Literal translation: It's on the deer's tail.

In a nutshell: Ever try to chase a deer? Don't try. They are the most elusive of creatures, so to grab something on their tails is impossible. This saying means "*to chase after the elusive, to chase rainbows*."

"Los pobladores confiaron su voto al alcalde electo, pero las promesas parecen haber quedado en '**la cola de un venado**.'" Translation: "Residents trusted their vote to the mayor elect, but those promises will *never* be kept."

estar que rasca

Literal meaning: to have
the urge to scratch

In a nutshell: A good number of animals
have the habit of scratching the ground
when they are anxious to get out of their
pens. The statement "**Estoy que rasco**"
means "*I've got the itch to [do something].*"

"Juan **está que rasca** por recibir un
nuevo chance." Translation: "Juan is *dying*
to get another chance."

THE ITCH TO SCRATCH

A similar word is **raspaditas**, which means literally
"*the things scratched.*" This refers to the local lot-
tery ticket, which has a series of numbers that only
become visible when a protective covering has been
scratched off.

pegar carreras

Literal meaning: to glue races

In a nutshell: This idiom means "*to be running around.*"

"Lo mejor es tomar algunas precauciones para evitar '**pegar carreras**' de última hora." Translation: "It's better to take precautions and avoid *running around* at the last minute." (See "**andar de Herodes a Pilato**," page 59.)

ponerse las pilas

Literal meaning: to put in the batteries

In a nutshell: When the batteries of your electronic devices run low, things almost come to a standstill. Pop some new ones in, and, *voilà*, they jump back to life! Figuratively, then, **ponerse las pilas** means "*to get on the ball, to work with renewed vigor.*"

"Cuando vi que la construcción se estaba atrasando, tuve que **ponerme las pilas**." Translation: "When I noticed that the construction was getting behind schedule, I really had *to get on the ball.*"

On the Road AGAIN

**Put on some traveling
music and head to
#173-179!**

SECTION 14

atollarse

to get stuck in the mud

"El camión quedó **atollado**." Translation: "The truck *got stuck in the mud*." The noun form is **atolladero**, "*mudhole*."

fulear

to fill

This is an obvious Anglicism, but quite common throughout the country. When you go to the gas station and the attendant asks you how much fuel you want, just say: "**Fuléamelo**." Translation: "*Fill it up*."

Similarly, if you are serving a meal to someone and you offer him a third plate of food, he's likely to say: "No, gracias. Estoy **ful**." Translation: "No, thanks. I'm *stuffed*."

160

en la ruta 11

Literal meaning: To be on [bus] route 11

In a nutshell: The local bus routes in Managua all have numbers, the 110, the 117, and so on. But when a person doesn't have the funds to take the bus, he takes "Route 11." This is because, when we are walking, from a distance the silhouettess of our two legs look like the number "11." If someone says: "Ando **en la ruta 11**," he is giving you the sad news that he has to walk.

By the way, *GringoGuide200* is offering a lifetime pass for Route 11 for only US$100! (If you believe this, you need to read again "**hacérsele el cambiolín**," page 79.)

guindo

(pronounced GEEN-doh)

a cliff, or figuratively, hill

"René se perdió en esos **guindos**." Translation: "René got lost out in those *hills*."

hacerse humo

Literal meaning: to become smoke

In a nutshell: After a fire has been put out, where does the smoke go? It simply disappears. If someone says: "**Me hice humo**," it means "*I hit the road*."

interlocal

a mini-van used in public transport

These mini-vans offer express service between major cities. But be careful. The drivers are known for their reckless maneuvers on the road, so much so that people jokingly call them **intermortales**, the wild transport that sometimes becomes *mortal.*

179

policía acostado

Literal meaning: a sleeping policeman

In a nutshell: An imaginative Nicaraguan, the first time he saw a speed bump, must have likened it to a sleeping policeman. And it stuck. Other countries use terms such as "túmulos" or "muertos," but this Nicaraguan masterpiece wins the price for creativity.

I was traveling by vehicle to a town in northern Nicaragua with some friends when we happened upon an unusually high speed bump. I remarked that I had never seen such a large **policía acostado**. My friend quipped: "Eso no es una **policía acostado**. ¡Es un **cocinero** acostado!" Translation: "That's not a *sleeping policeman*. That's a sleeping *cook!*"

WATCH OUT OR THEY WILL REEL YOU IN!
By the way, informally police are referred to as **la pesca**, which means something like *"the fishermen."* When they stop you and explain the supposed infraction you've committed, they will ask for some money for **gaseosas**, the term for *"sodas."*

All in a day's Work

All work and no play
made Jack a dull boy.
See why in #180-194!

SECTION 15

a mecate corto

Literal meaning: at a short rope

to have someone under control

"Hay que mantener a ese chavalo **a mecate corto**." Translation: "Make sure you *keep* that guy *in check*."

bisnear

This comes from English, meaning "*to do business*." In Chinandega, one market area is known as "**El Bisne**."

"¿Dónde aprendió la Elena a **bisnear**?" Translation: "Where did Elena learn how *to wheel and deal*?"

a medio palo

Literal meaning: at half stick

In a nutshell: The phrase means to leave something unfinished or halfway done. Due to the poor economy, many homes are left **a medio palo**, perhaps with just a few walls in place. Originally, this saying may have had reference to the mast of ships. If the sails were lowered to half mast, the speed would be reduced considerably.

"Juan estaba construyendo su casa, pero le quedó **a medio palo.**" Translation: "Juan started building his home, but it was left *unfinished.*"

a tuto

Literal meaning: unknown

In a nutshell: This means "*to carry on your back*" and figuratively "*to shoulder responsibility.*"

"Tuvimos que sacar la cosecha **a tuto**." Translation: "We had to get the harvest out *by carrying it on our backs*." Figuratively one might say: "Llevo cuatro chavalos **a tuto**." Translation: "I'm *caring for* four children."

cancanear

to stutter or read poorly

Person A: "¿Sabes leer?"
Person B: "Solo puedo medio **cancanear**."

Translation: "Do you know how to read?"
"I can *barely stutter* a few words."

chapiollo

of poor quality

"Estos albañiles hacen trabajos **chapiollos**." Translation: "These masons only do *garbage work*."

Other very informal adjectives that define something of poor quality are **chanfaina** and **champú**.

chiche

easy

"No es tan **chiche** cambiar de empleo." Translation: "It's not so *easy* to change jobs."

cuerear

to be difficult

"Evitar comer cosas grasosas me **cuerea**."
Translation: "Avoiding eating fatty foods *is really hard* for me."

desrengado

tattered; disheveled

One fellow was complimented on the shirt he was wearing, and his response was: "¡Qué va a ser! Tengo años de usar esta pobrecita **desrengada**!" Translation: "You've got to be kidding me! I've been using this *tattered old* thing for years."

desarme

Literal meaning: "the place where things are taken apart."

It's the everyday word for a "*junkyard.*" The difference between these junkyards and their counterparts overseas is that most of the vehicles have been dismantled and categorically separated.

IF YOUR CAR BREAKS DOWN...

Auto parts here are called **repuestos**, and not "refacciones" as in other Latin countries. If you get a flat tire, just try to make it to a **vulcanización**, a small roadside tire shop, where you will be up and running for just a few córdobas. The sign for these places is a huge tire planted in the front yard, upon which the word **VULCANIZACIÓN** has been scrawled.

echar la vaca

Literal meaning: to throw the cow

In a nutshell: In case you haven't noticed, cows are pretty heavy animals. To throw one, you would need the New York Giants' entire defensive line. But when many people unite for a common cause, their collective power can be a force to reckon with. If someone says: "**Me echaron la vaca**," it's as if to say: "*They're all ganging up on me.*"

El que mucho abarca, poco aprieta.

Literal translation: He who
encompasses much, squeezes little.

In a nutshell: Ever try to eat more than you could chew, or take on a project that was beyond your strength? If so, you can relate to this saying. Try this: put a golf ball in your hand and squeeze as hard as you can. Now, put three balls in your hand, and squeeze again. In which instance do you have a better grip? The answer is obvious. The lesson? The more things we are juggling in our lives, the less control we have over them. This pearl of wisdom is often uttered after analyzing why a particular project is not going as planned.

One opinion writer lamented: "'**El que mucho abarca poco aprieta**' es el refrán popular que mejor define el resultado de la visita de cinco días de Barack Obama a América Latina." Translation: "'*Don't spread yourself too thin*' is the popular saying that best defines Barack Obama's five-day visit to Latin America." [The implication is that little was accomplished because so little time was dedicated.]

Después del gustazo, el trancazo.

Literal meaning: After having a great time, you get hit with a large wooden beam.

In a nutshell: As a protection against thieves, some homes have a **tranca**, or *large wooden beam*, which sits on wooden hooks just inside the closed interior doors, like a giant latch. The action of hitting someone with one of those huge beams is called a **trancazo**. Sometimes after enjoying ourselves, perhaps after being on vacation, we must go back to the grind, or even be the victim of some tragedy.

"**Después de un gustazo un trancazo**, eso fue lo que literalmente les pasó a ocho jóvenes que ayer viajaban en una camioneta que se volcó." Translation: "*Tragedy after pleasure*, that's literally what happened to eight young people who were traveling yesterday when a pick-up truck flipped over."

¡Muerta la lora, y que nadie la llore!

Literal meaning: Death to the parrot, and may no one mourn her!

In a nutshell: When a job of any sort is finished, the proud worker will jubilantly exclaim these words. In Great Britain in similar circumstances, some people say: "*...and Bob's your uncle.*" It's similar to saying: "*It's a done deal.*"

EVEN OUR NOSES HAVE LATCHES
(from previous page)
Figuratively, even parts of our bodies can be closed in this way. If someone says: "**Estoy trancado**," he probably has a cold and is congested. Similarly, **volarse las trancas**, "*flying over the latches*," means that someone has taken matters into his own hands, bypassing normal procedures.

Sin dinero
no baila el mono.

Literal meaning: Without money the monkey doesn't dance.

In a nutshell: Imagine the circus monkey. He'll do a lot of cute tricks for you... for a price! Some of our primate friends were trained under the arrangement of tricks for money. No money, no tricks. So when someone tells you "**Sin dinero, no baila el mono**," they are saying they are *not willing to work for free.*

"Cuando le pregunté a William si podía podar algunos arboles en mi patio, me dijo: "**Sin dinero, no baila el mono**." Translation: "When I asked William if he would prune some trees in my yard, he responded: "*No money, no work.*"

A little Personality

**Avoid vanilla!
Show some flair! See how
in #195-200!**

SECTION 16

chachalaca

Literal meaning: a raucous type of bird

However, it is more often used figuratively to denote someone who is *a big talker*.

"Con la Julia cuesta hablar uno. ¡Qué clase de **chachalaca**!" Translation: "It's so hard to get a word in with Julia. You should see what a *big talker* she is!"

chichicaste

Literal meaning: a type of worm

Watch out! Touch one of these creatures and you get a terrible burning sensation on your skin. Figuratively, it refers to *an easily irritated person.*

"Chilo, no seas **chichicaste**. No te quisieron ofender." Translation: "Chilo, don't be *so sensitive*. They weren't trying to offend you." Someone described as a **delicado** will likewise have his feelings hurt at the drop of a hat.

fachento

stuck up

Having an air of superiority. A person who is **fachento** tries to pass as being in a higher class than he really is. Even so, the word is often used jokingly. "Mirá, ¡qué bonitos tus nuevos zapatos! ¡Andás **fachenta**!" Translation: "Hey, I love your new shoes! *Aren't we high class?*" **Jayán** is another similar term, but with a decidedly negative connotation. It means "*conceited*" or even "*rude*."

THE HIGH CLASS BEAN DINNER

Founded way back in 1524 by Francisco Hernández de Córdoba, Granada has staked its claim to being the oldest city in the Americas and is the town most visited by tourists. Because of its traditional prominence, those outside the city have always painted the Granadians as having an air of superiority. Yes, they are **fachentos**! One joke goes like this: "Los granadinos son tan **fachentos** que cuando comen frijoles, eruptan pollo." Translation: "The Granadians are so *stuck up* that even when they eat beans, they burp chicken." Boy, I wonder what they are putting in those beans!

Mamacita de Tarzán

Literal meaning: Tarzan's mommy

If Tarzan was a force to be reckoned with, you can bet his mamma was no slouch either. This colorful term refers to someone who thinks he or she can solve any problem.

A blogger complaining about the lack of taxis in his town wrote: "Así que necesitamos más taxis, porque los que están se las dan de la **Mamacita de Tarzán** y no son ni el puñal." Translation: "And so we need more taxis, because the ones we have put on airs as if they were *Tarzan's mommy*; they're not even [as strong as] his dagger." Ouch!

dejado

a failure

When Donald Trump and Rosie O'Donnell began a much-publicized war of words, the business magnate's disparaging comments about her were translated this way in the Nicaraguan press. "Dijo que el aspecto de la actriz era 'asqueroso tanto por fuera como por dentro. Mírala, es una **dejada**.'" Translation: "He said that the actress' appearance was 'disgusting both inside as well as outside. Look at her, she's a *failure*.'"

matamama

Literal meaning: mamma killer

A traitor. "Yo también creo que no hay que ser **mata-mama**. Los nicas debemos aprender a valorar y proteger lo nuestro." Translation: "I also believe *we shouldn't bite the hand that feeds us*. As Nicaraguans we must learn to value and protect our own."

The Golden Ipegüe

Congratulations! You are now a bona fide Nicaraguan Spanish speaker. You are the proud owner of 200 of the the country's best words, phrases, and sayings. Here's one more on the house!

The Golden
IPEGÜE

uno más del Taller Cajina

Literal meaning: one more from Cajina's shop

In a nutshell: In the city of Boaco, there is a famous shop that makes **camastros**, or enclosed beds for cattle trucks. These are then painted in bright colors and the shop stencils its signature sign on the back, giving itself free publicity: **UNO MÁS DEL TALLER CAJINA, BOACO**. Since the cattle industry plays a prominent role in the Nicaraguan economy, there are thousands of these trucks on the road.

They are so common that people get sick of seeing them. It reminds me of McDonald's, which used to boast about how many millions and even trillions of hamburgers they had served. After so many, you lose count, and people really don't care anymore. For that reason, "**Uno más del Taller Cajina**" has come to mean "*the same old thing*" or "*here we go again.*"

"Nada de cambio, **uno más del Taller Cajina**."
Translation: "There's never any change.
It's always the same old thing."

Forgot what an **ipegüe** *is? Go back to page 146.*

Index

Made in the USA
San Bernardino, CA
15 September 2014